FULFILLING
LEADERSHIP
The 5 Pillars

Ricardo Donath

DEDICATION

To Kym, Raphi, Yony, and Elke, my why.

CONTENTS

ACKNOWLEDGMENT

I would like to express my deepest gratitude to all the individuals who have overcome tremendous hardships and generously shared their knowledge and experiences with the world. Your resilience, wisdom, and willingness to impart your valuable insights have been instrumental in shaping the ideas presented in this book.

To the trailblazers who have paved the way for others, thank you for your courage and determination. Your stories of triumph over adversity have inspired countless individuals to persevere and strive for greatness.

I am indebted to the mentors and teachers who have guided me on my own journey of growth and learning. Your guidance, support, and unwavering belief in my potential have been invaluable.

To the researchers and thought leaders who have dedicated their lives to understanding the complexities of leadership and personal fulfillment, thank you for your tireless efforts in advancing our understanding of these crucial areas.

I would also like to extend my gratitude to the readers and listeners who have embraced the concepts and ideas shared in this book. Your curiosity, engagement, and feedback have been instrumental in shaping its final form.

Lastly, I want to express my heartfelt appreciation to my family, friends, and loved ones for their unwavering support and encouragement throughout this journey. Your belief in me and your constant presence have been a source of strength and inspiration.

PROLOGUE

In the depths of my being, there has always been an unwavering passion for leadership. From a young age, I found myself drawn to the intricacies of guiding and inspiring others towards a common purpose. Little did I know that this passion would take me on a transformative journey, shaping not only my understanding of leadership but also my personal growth and fulfillment.

My path toward fulfilling leadership had an influential period during my time in the army and the security service, specifically, the diplomatic security service. These experiences exposed me to the immense power and responsibility that comes with leading in high-stakes environments. I witnessed firsthand the impact that effective leadership can have on individuals, teams, and the successful accomplishment of missions. It was during these formative years that I realized the true potential of leadership to shape lives and create positive change.

However, my journey was not without its challenges. Alongside my pursuit of leadership excellence, I faced a personal battle with depression and anxiety. These invisible adversaries threatened to undermine my confidence, hinder my ability to connect with others, and dampen my leadership potential. It was during this dark period that I discovered the transformative power of the five pillars of fulfilling leadership.

Service to others and a purpose became my guiding light, reminding me of the importance of looking beyond myself and finding meaning in making a positive impact on others. Through acts of service, I found solace and a renewed sense of purpose that propelled me forward.

Taking care of my physical and mental well-being became paramount. I recognized the profound connection between a healthy diet, regular exercise, and my overall sense of well-being. Nourishing my body and mind allowed me to regain strength, clarity, and resilience, enabling me to face the challenges of leadership with renewed vigor.

Sticking to the mission and striving for victory became my mantra. I learned to set clear goals, maintain focus, and persevere through adversity. The pursuit of victory was not merely about achieving success but about embracing the journey and the growth it entailed.

Leading by example became my compass, guiding me toward authenticity, integrity, and empathy. I understood that my actions spoke louder than words, and by embodying the qualities I sought in others, I could inspire and empower those around me.

Through the application and experience of these five pillars, I not only overcame my struggles but also witnessed a profound transformation in my leadership skills. As I embraced fulfilling leadership, I discovered a newfound sense of purpose, fulfillment, and connection with those I led.

In my quest for fulfilling leadership, I not only drew inspiration from my experiences in the military and the security services but also sought to integrate the timeless principles of military leadership into the broader framework of fulfilling leadership. The military has long been a crucible for developing effective leaders and honing their skills in high-pressure situations where lives and missions are at stake.

From the military, I learned the importance of discipline, resilience, and adaptability. These principles, forged in the crucible of combat and adversity, have a profound impact on leadership effectiveness. By incorporating these principles into the fabric of fulfilling leadership, we can navigate the complexities of the modern world with strength, agility, and unwavering determination.

The military also instilled in me a deep sense of duty, honor, and selfless service. These values, rooted in the military ethos, form the bedrock of fulfilling leadership. By embracing the principles of service to others and a purpose, we can transcend self-interest and elevate our leadership to a higher calling, one that seeks to make a positive impact on the lives of those we lead and the world we inhabit.

In this book, I aim to bridge the gap between military leadership and the broader context of fulfilling leadership. By integrating the principles and lessons learned from the military with the five pillars of fulfilling leadership, we can forge a comprehensive approach that encompasses the best of both worlds. This fusion of military leadership principles with the broader framework of fulfilling leadership creates a powerful synergy, enabling us to navigate the complexities of the modern world while staying true to our purpose and values.

This book is a testament to my journey, a journey that has taught me the true essence of fulfilling leadership. It is a collection of insights, inspiring stories, academic research, and practical strategies that I have gathered along the way. It is my hope that by sharing my experiences and knowledge, I can inspire and empower others to embark on their own path of fulfilling leadership to overcome their own obstacles, and to make a positive impact in their spheres of influence.

Join me as we delve into the depths of fulfilling leadership, exploring the power it holds to transform lives, organizations, and the world at large. Together, let us embark on a journey of growth, purpose, and fulfillment, as we unlock the true potential of leadership within ourselves and those we serve.

WHAT IS FULFILLING LEADERSHIP?

Fulfilling leadership is a concept that goes beyond traditional notions of authority and power. It encompasses a holistic approach to leadership that focuses on creating a positive and meaningful impact on individuals, teams, organizations, and society as a whole. At its core, fulfilling leadership is about inspiring and empowering others to reach their full potential, fostering a sense of purpose, and promoting well-being.

Fulfilling leadership starts with self-awareness and a deep understanding of one's values, strengths, and passions. A fulfilling leader aligns their personal purpose with the goals and values of the organization, creating a sense of shared purpose and meaning. They lead by example, demonstrating authenticity, integrity, and empathy in their interactions.

One of the key aspects of fulfilling leadership is the emphasis on building strong relationships and fostering a culture of trust and collaboration. A fulfilling leader recognizes the importance of valuing and respecting the diverse perspectives and contributions of team members. They create an inclusive environment where everyone feels heard, valued, and empowered to contribute their best.

A fulfilling leader also prioritizes the growth and development of their team members. They provide mentorship, guidance, and opportunities for learning and advancement. By investing in the personal and professional growth of others, they create a supportive and nurturing environment that encourages continuous improvement and fosters a sense of fulfillment.

In addition to focusing on the well-being and growth of individuals, fulfilling leadership extends to the broader community and society. A fulfilling leader recognizes their responsibility to make a positive impact beyond the confines of their organization. They actively engage in social and environmental initiatives, promoting sustainability, diversity, and social justice.

Ultimately, fulfilling leadership is about creating a harmonious balance between achieving organizational goals and nurturing the well-being and fulfillment of individuals. It is a leadership style that inspires, motivates, and empowers others to reach their highest potential while making a positive difference in the world. By embracing fulfilling leadership, individuals and organizations can create a culture of purpose, fulfillment, and sustainable success.

THE 5 PILLARS

The five pillars of fulfilling leadership - service to others and a purpose, diet, stick to the mission and strive for victory, exercise, and lead by example - serve as the foundation of fulfilling leadership. They provide a solid framework upon which other traits, behaviors, and aspects of leadership and fulfillment can be built. By embracing and integrating these pillars into our lives and leadership styles, we establish a strong base from which to grow and develop.

The five pillars lay the groundwork for fulfilling leadership by addressing key areas that contribute to our overall well-being and effectiveness as leaders. Service to others and a purpose fosters a sense of meaning and connection, while diet and exercise support our physical and mental health. Sticking to the mission and striving for victory inspires focus and determination, and leading by example builds trust and credibility.

Once these pillars become an embedded part of our lives and leadership styles, they create a solid foundation upon which we can further develop other important traits and behaviors. For example, effective communication, emotional intelligence, adaptability, and resilience can be cultivated and strengthened on top of the foundation provided by the five pillars. These additional aspects of leadership and fulfillment can be built upon the strong base established by the pillars, enhancing our overall leadership effectiveness and personal fulfillment.

By recognizing the importance of the five pillars and making them an integral part of our lives, we create a solid foundation that supports our growth as leaders. As we continue to develop and refine our leadership skills and behaviors, we can build upon this foundation, expanding our capacity to inspire, empower, and make a positive impact on others.

Service to Others and to a Purpose: Service to others and a purpose involves prioritizing the well-being and success of others, as well as aligning our actions with a greater mission. By focusing on serving others, we create a positive impact on individuals, teams, and communities. This pillar fosters empathy, collaboration, and a sense of shared purpose, leading to stronger relationships, higher engagement, and a more fulfilling leadership experience.

Diet: Diet refers not only to the food we consume but also to the mental and emotional nourishment we provide ourselves. A healthy diet, both physically and mentally, is essential for sustaining our energy, focus, and overall well-being. Proper nutrition, mindfulness practices, and self-care routines contribute to increased resilience, mental clarity, and emotional balance, enabling us to lead with greater effectiveness and fulfillment.

Stick to the Mission and Strive for Victory: Staying committed to the mission and striving for victory involves setting clear goals, maintaining focus, and persevering through challenges. By aligning our actions with the mission, we create a sense of purpose and direction. This pillar encourages resilience, determination, and a growth mindset, allowing us to overcome obstacles, inspire others, and experience a sense of fulfillment when we achieve our objectives.

Exercise: Regular physical exercise is vital for maintaining optimal health, energy levels, and mental well-being. Engaging in physical activity boosts our mood, reduces stress, and enhances cognitive function. As leaders, exercise helps us manage stress, increase productivity, and maintain a positive mindset. It also sets an example for others, promoting a culture of well-being and self-care within our teams.

Lead by Example: Leading by example is about embodying the values, behaviors, and qualities we expect from others. It involves demonstrating integrity, authenticity, and accountability in our actions. When we lead by example, we inspire trust, motivate others, and create a positive work culture. This pillar fosters respect, credibility, and a sense of purpose, leading to greater fulfillment as we see the positive impact we have on others.

While these five pillars are essential, it's important to note that leadership and fulfillment are multifaceted and require a balance of various traits, behaviors, and aspects. Each individual may have their own unique combination of strengths and areas for growth. By recognizing and developing these different aspects, we can cultivate a well-rounded leadership approach that promotes both personal and collective fulfillment. Once these pillars are embedded in our lives and leadership styles, we can further cultivate and enhance other important traits and behaviors, creating a well-rounded approach to leadership that promotes both personal and collective fulfillment.

PILLAR I - SERVICE

In the context of leadership, fulfillment, and the military, serving others refers to the act of prioritizing the well-being, growth, and success of those under your leadership. It involves putting the needs of others before your own and actively working to support and empower them. This can include providing guidance, mentorship, resources, and opportunities for development. Serving others as a leader involves fostering a culture of collaboration, empathy, and support, where individuals feel valued, heard, and motivated to contribute their best.

Serving a higher purpose, on the other hand, involves aligning your leadership efforts with a greater cause or mission that goes beyond personal gain. It means recognizing that your role as a leader extends beyond achieving individual or organizational success and includes making a positive impact on a larger scale. This higher purpose can be driven by values, principles, or a desire to create meaningful change in the world. It provides a sense of direction, inspiration, and a deeper meaning to your leadership journey.

In the military, serving others and serving a higher purpose are fundamental aspects of leadership. Military leaders are entrusted with the responsibility of leading and protecting their teams, often in high-stakes and challenging environments. Serving others in the military involves ensuring the well-being, safety, and development of the individuals under their command. It means putting the mission and the welfare of the team above personal interests.

Serving a higher purpose in the military often revolves around the mission and values of the military organization itself. It involves dedicating oneself to the defense and protection of one's country and upholding the principles of justice, freedom, and security. Military leaders understand that their actions have a direct impact on the lives of their fellow service members, as well as the communities they serve.

While serving in the military I learned what makes a leader great and it all starts with service to others and service to a higher purpose. A service that goes beyond your personal needs. During that time, I was fulfilled, despite the hard work, risk, and danger, the intrinsic contentment was at its highest. We did not have many extrinsic gratifications or recognitions probably because no one knew what we did but the feeling of knowing that others were better off because the work that we did was astonishing.

Why is important to have service at the center of our leadership practices?

When leaders prioritize service to others, they foster a culture of empathy, collaboration, and trust within their teams. By genuinely caring for the well-being and growth of their team members, leaders create strong relationships based on mutual respect and support. This, in turn, leads to increased employee engagement, loyalty, and productivity.

Leaders who serve others and embody a higher purpose inspire and motivate their team members. When individuals see their leaders selflessly working towards a greater cause, it ignites a sense of purpose and meaning in their own work. This can lead to increased motivation, dedication, and a shared commitment to achieving organizational goals.

Service-oriented leaders prioritize creating a positive work culture where individuals feel valued, appreciated, and supported. By fostering an environment of collaboration, inclusivity, and personal growth, leaders can enhance employee satisfaction and well-being. This, in turn, contributes to higher levels of engagement, creativity, and overall fulfillment within the organization.

Leaders who serve a higher cause understand that their actions have the potential to make a lasting impact beyond their immediate sphere of influence. By aligning their leadership with a purpose that transcends personal gain, leaders can contribute to positive change in their communities, industries, or even the world. This sense of making a difference can bring a deep sense of fulfillment and satisfaction to leaders.

Engaging in service to others and a higher cause can be personally transformative for leaders. It allows them to develop a broader perspective, cultivate empathy, and tap into their own values and passions. By aligning their leadership with their personal values and a greater purpose, leaders can experience a deeper sense of fulfillment, meaning, and personal growth.

Service to others and service to a higher cause are important in leadership and fulfillment because they foster strong relationships, inspire and motivate others, create a positive work culture, make a lasting impact, and contribute to personal growth and fulfillment. By embracing these principles, leaders can create a positive ripple effect that extends beyond their immediate circle of influence and leads to a more fulfilling and impactful leadership journey.

Academic Research

From an academic research perspective, the importance and effects of service to others and service to a higher purpose on leadership and fulfillment have been extensively studied. Here are some key points, along with corresponding academic research supporting each point:

Enhanced Leadership Effectiveness: Academic studies, such as those by Liden et al. (2008) and Bolger et al. (2000), have consistently shown that leaders who prioritize service to others and a higher purpose are more effective in inspiring and motivating their teams. By focusing on the well-being and success of others, these leaders create a positive work environment, enhance employee well-being, and foster organizational success.

Increased Employee Engagement and Satisfaction: Research, including studies by Liden et al. (2008) and Bolger et al. (2000), has highlighted that leaders who prioritize service to others and a higher purpose contribute to higher levels of employee engagement and satisfaction. When employees feel that their work has a meaningful impact and aligns with a greater purpose, they are more likely to be motivated, committed, and fulfilled in their roles.

Positive Organizational Culture: Academic studies, such as those by Liden et al. (2008) and Damon et al. (2003), have shown that leaders who prioritize service to others and a higher purpose play a crucial role in shaping a positive organizational culture. By fostering a culture of collaboration, empathy, and shared values, these leaders create an environment where individuals feel valued, supported, and fulfilled.

Personal Fulfillment and Well-being: Research, including studies by Steger et al. (2012) and Damon et al. (2003), has highlighted that individuals who prioritize service to others and a higher purpose experience higher levels of personal fulfillment and well-being. By aligning their actions with a greater mission, individuals find a sense of meaning, purpose, and satisfaction in their work, leading to increased overall well-being.

Positive Impact on Society: Academic studies, such as those by Liden et al. (2008) and Damon et al. (2003), have emphasized that service to others and a higher-purpose leadership have a positive impact on society. By focusing on the greater good and contributing to the well-being of communities, these leaders inspire others to make a difference and create a positive social impact.

These academic studies provide robust evidence supporting the importance and effects of service to others and service to a higher purpose on leadership and fulfillment. By prioritizing these principles, leaders can enhance their effectiveness, create a positive work environment, increase employee engagement and satisfaction, foster personal fulfillment and well-being, and make a positive impact on society as a whole.

Inspiring Stories
Patagonia
Patagonia is a renowned outdoor clothing and gear company that has become a shining example of how a focus on service to others and service to a purpose can make an organization great. Patagonia's commitment to environmental sustainability and social responsibility has been at the core of its business model. By prioritizing the well-being of the planet and its communities, Patagonia has not only built a loyal customer base but has also inspired a movement toward conscious consumerism.

Through initiatives like the "1% for the Planet" campaign, Patagonia donates a portion of its sales to environmental causes. The company also encourages customers to repair their products rather than replace them, reducing waste and promoting a culture of durability. By aligning its purpose with the greater good, Patagonia has created a strong brand identity and a sense of purpose that resonates with employees, customers, and stakeholders alike.

Southwest Airlines
Southwest Airlines is widely recognized for its exceptional customer service and employee-centric culture. The airline's success can be attributed to its unwavering commitment to service to others. Southwest Airlines places a strong emphasis on creating a positive experience for both customers and employees, fostering a sense of community and care.

By prioritizing the well-being of its employees, Southwest Airlines ensures that they are motivated, engaged, and empowered to deliver exceptional service. The company's unique approach to customer service, such as open seating and no baggage fees, sets it apart from competitors and creates a more inclusive and enjoyable travel experience. Southwest Airlines' dedication to service has earned it a loyal customer base and a reputation for being a people-oriented organization.

Virgin Group

The Virgin Group, led by entrepreneur Richard Branson, is a conglomerate of companies spanning various industries, including travel, entertainment, and telecommunications. What sets Virgin Group apart is its relentless focus on service to others and service to a purpose. Branson has always emphasized the importance of putting customers first and creating innovative solutions to meet their needs.

Virgin Group's success can be attributed to its ability to disrupt traditional industries by offering unique and customer-centric experiences. Whether it's Virgin Atlantic's personalized in-flight service or Virgin Galactic's ambitious space tourism venture, the group consistently strives to exceed customer expectations. By infusing a sense of purpose and a commitment to service into each of its ventures, Virgin Group has built a strong brand that stands for quality, innovation, and customer satisfaction.

In summary, organizations like Patagonia, Southwest Airlines, and Virgin Group have achieved greatness by embracing service to others and service to a purpose. By prioritizing the well-being of their customers, employees, and the greater community, these organizations have not only built successful businesses but have also made a positive impact on society. Their commitment to service has created a sense of purpose, loyalty, and admiration among stakeholders, setting them apart as leaders in their respective industries.

Practical ways to introduce service into our leadership practices.

Now we know that Incorporating service to others and service to a higher purpose into your organization can have a profound impact on employee engagement, organizational culture, and overall success. Here are some practical ways to put these principles into practice:

1. Clearly articulate and communicate the higher purpose of our organization. This purpose should go beyond financial goals and focus on making a positive impact on society or a specific cause. Leaders must Ensure that all employees understand and connect with this purpose.

2. Lead by example by embodying the values and behaviors associated

with these principles. Show genuine care for their employees, customers, and the community.

3. Create an environment that empowers employees to serve others and contribute to the higher purpose. Encourage them to identify ways they can make a positive impact within their roles and provide them with the autonomy and resources to do so.

4. Build a culture that encourages collaboration, teamwork, and support among employees. Encourage cross-functional collaboration and create opportunities for employees to work together on projects that align with the organization's higher purpose.

5. Acknowledge and reward employees who demonstrate a commitment to serving others and contributing to the higher purpose. Not only results but also how much they contribute to the cause.

6. Incorporate service-oriented goals and metrics into performance evaluations. Again, not only metrics that are result-based. This will reinforce the importance of service to others and a higher purpose and ensure that employees' contributions in these areas are recognized and valued.

7. Encourage employees and followers to participate in community service initiatives aligned with the organization's higher purpose. This can involve volunteering, fundraising, or partnering with local organizations to address social or environmental issues.

8. Regularly seek feedback from employees, customers, and stakeholders to assess the impact of the organization's service-oriented efforts. You can use this feedback to make improvements and refine your approach over time.

Remember, implementing the practical ways for service is an ongoing process that requires commitment and consistency. By integrating these principles into your organization's values, culture, and most importantly practices, you can create a positive and purpose-driven workplace that benefits yourself, your employees, and the broader community.

PILLAR II - DIET

Why Diet is important for leadership and fulfillment? It is because it directly impacts our physical and mental well-being. A balanced wholefood diet provides the necessary nutrients for optimal brain function, energy levels, and emotional stability, enabling people and leaders to think clearly, make sound decisions, and effectively manage stress. A balanced diet also supports overall health, reducing the risk of chronic diseases and promoting longevity. By prioritizing a healthy diet, leaders can set an example, inspire others, and create a positive culture of well-being, ultimately enhancing their own fulfillment and the success of their journeys.

When it comes to my personal nutritional experience, in the past I had a fluctuating pattern of healthy and unhealthy diets, not fully realizing the impact they had on my well-being, especially my mental health. When I was younger, I didn't notice the immediate effects, but as I grew older, I began to experience a decline in my performance as a leader, accompanied by feelings of anxiety, depression, and low energy, not knowing that these symptoms were linked partly to my poor dietary choices.

Additionally, I used to cope with stress by turning to food, especially sugary foods to seek comfort and the release of the pleasure hormone, dopamine, to counteract the effects of the stress hormone, cortisol. After feeling depressed, anxious, and with no energy for a while, I studied the effects of the Western diet which is very high on refined carbohydrates, and how it directly influenced my physical and mental state. That exploration led me to adopt a high fat low carbohydrate diet.

I would like to mention that in this chapter we will explore what happens to our bodies when we eat. It's important to say that while I will be focusing on the effects of eating, I acknowledge the significance and importance of what happens in the body when we fast.

What happens in the body when we eat?

Once glucose, fatty acids, or amino acids enter the cells, they undergo a series of chemical reactions in the mitochondria, known as cellular respiration. This process converts these molecules into adenosine triphosphate (ATP), which is the energy currency of the body. Energy can also be created using stored fat which is a much more efficient source of energy. ATP is then used by cells to perform various functions, including muscle contraction, nerve signaling, and biochemical reactions. If the chemical reaction in the mitochondria is not fuelled with the right kind of macronutrients, the chemical reactions will not be efficient.

Insulin

Insulin is the hormone produced by the pancreas that plays a crucial role in regulating blood sugar levels. When we consume carbohydrates, especially those that are quickly digested and high in sugar or refined carbohydrates, our blood sugar levels rise. In response, the pancreas releases insulin into the bloodstream. Insulin acts as a key that unlocks cells, allowing glucose to enter and be used as a source of energy. This process helps lower blood sugar levels and maintain them within a healthy range. However, when we consume excessive amounts of carbohydrates or have insulin resistance, the body may produce more insulin to compensate. This can lead to chronically elevated insulin levels, which can have various effects on metabolism, weight management, and overall health.

Elevated insulin levels, often associated with conditions like insulin resistance or type 2 diabetes, can have negative health effects. It can lead to imbalances in blood sugar levels, increased fat storage, and other metabolic diseases.

Refined and Simple Carbohydrates

Unfortunately, these days, the Western diet is characterized by high amounts of refined carbohydrates and sugars. Here we explore some of the effects of diets high in refined and simple carbohydrates.

Carbohydrates can contribute to weight gain, obesity, and an increased risk of related health conditions such as diabetes, heart disease, and certain cancers.

Many processed foods contain pro-inflammatory ingredients such as refined sugars, unhealthy fats, and artificial additives. Chronic inflammation is associated with various health issues, including mental health disorders like depression and anxiety.

A diet high in processed foods has been linked to cognitive decline and impaired brain function. These foods lack essential nutrients, antioxidants, and healthy fats that are crucial for brain health and cognitive performance.

The lack of nutrients and the presence of unhealthy additives may disrupt neurotransmitter balance and negatively impact mood regulation.

Processed foods often provide quick bursts of energy due to their high sugar content. However, this energy is short-lived and followed by crashes, leading to fatigue, decreased productivity, and difficulty concentrating.

Processed foods are typically low in fiber, which is essential for a healthy digestive system. This can lead to digestive problems such as constipation, bloating, and an imbalance in gut bacteria, which has been linked to mental health issues.

What is the Recommended diet these days?

In the past, we were often advised to eat carbohydrates and avoid saturated fats, now we know that healthy saturated fats do not necessarily contribute to weight gain, and it is the quality, quantity, and frequency of our overall diet that plays a more significant role. As we just mentioned, processed carbohydrates have been identified as a key factor in weight gain and the increase of chronic diseases. Based on this, adopting a high-fat/low-carbohydrate diet is now recommended as a beneficial approach to promoting not only weight management but overall health.

How can a low-carbohydrate diet impact us as leaders?

Refined sugars and carbohydrates can cause energy crashes and brain fog, leading to decreased productivity and focus. By reducing these sources of quick energy, a low carbohydrate diet can help stabilize energy levels and promote mental clarity, allowing individuals to perform at their best and make sound decisions.

The consumption of refined sugars and carbohydrates can lead to fluctuations in blood sugar levels, which can impact mood and emotional stability. By following a low carbohydrate diet, individuals may experience more stable blood sugar levels, which can contribute to improved mood, reduced mood swings, and increased emotional well-being.

Adopting a low-carbohydrate diet requires conscious decision-making and self-discipline at least at the beginning. By committing to this dietary approach, individuals can develop and strengthen their self-discipline and willpower, which are valuable qualities for personal growth and leadership.

As a leader, the choices we make, including our dietary habits, can have a significant impact on those around us. By following a low-carbohydrate diet and prioritizing health and well-being, we can serve as positive role models for our team and community. Our commitment to personal health can inspire others to make healthier choices and create a culture of well-being.

A low carbohydrate diet that focuses on whole, nutrient-dense foods can contribute to long-term health and vitality. By reducing the consumption of refined sugars and carbohydrates, individuals may lower their risk of chronic diseases such as obesity, type 2 diabetes, and heart disease. This can lead to a higher quality of life, increased longevity, and the ability to lead and inspire others for years to come.

Academic Research

While there is limited research specifically focusing on the effects of a low carbohydrate diet on leadership and fulfillment, there are studies that highlight the potential benefits of such a diet on cognitive function, mood, overall well-being, and other aspects such as:

Stable Energy Levels: Research suggests that a low carbohydrate diet can help stabilize blood sugar levels, providing a steady supply of energy throughout the day. This can contribute to improved focus, mental clarity, and sustained energy levels, which are essential for effective leadership and overall fulfillment.

Weight Management: Some studies indicate that a low carbohydrate diet may be effective for weight management. By reducing carbohydrate intake and focusing on nutrient-dense foods, individuals may experience weight loss or maintenance. Achieving and maintaining a healthy weight can positively impact self-confidence, well-being, and overall fulfillment.

Mental Well-being: While more research is needed, some studies suggest that a low carbohydrate diet may have positive effects on mental well-being. It is hypothesized that reducing carbohydrate intake and increasing healthy fats and proteins may support brain health and mood regulation. Improved mental well-being can contribute to enhanced leadership skills and overall fulfillment.

Metabolic Health: Research indicates that a low carbohydrate diet can have positive effects on metabolic health markers such as blood pressure, blood sugar levels, and cholesterol levels. By promoting metabolic health, individuals may experience improved overall well-being, which can positively impact leadership effectiveness and personal fulfillment.

Individual Variability: It's important to note that the effects of a low carbohydrate diet can vary among individuals. Factors such as genetics, overall diet quality, and individual health conditions can influence the outcomes. Consulting with a healthcare professional or registered dietitian is recommended to ensure a well-rounded and personalized approach to nutrition.

Inspiring Story
Dr. Chris Palmer is a psychiatrist and researcher at Harvard Medical School who has conducted studies on the effects of ketogenic diets on mental health conditions such as bipolar disorder and schizophrenia. His research has shown the benefits of low carbohydrate diets in improving symptoms and overall well-being.

Dr. Palmer's journey towards adopting a diet-based approach to treating mental health issues began after years of utilizing standard treatments for his patients. As a psychiatrist, he witnessed the limitations and challenges associated with traditional pharmacological interventions. Recognizing the need for alternative approaches, Dr. Palmer explored the emerging field of nutritional psychiatry.

Through his research and clinical experience, Dr. Palmer became intrigued by the potential impact of diet on mental health. He observed that many psychiatric disorders were associated with metabolic dysregulation and inflammation, leading him to explore the ketogenic diet as a potential therapeutic tool.

The ketogenic diet, characterized by a low carbohydrate intake and high fat consumption, aims to shift the body's metabolism into a state of ketosis. This metabolic state relies on ketones, produced from fat breakdown, as an alternative fuel source for the brain. Dr. Palmer assumed that this dietary approach could positively influence brain function and potentially alleviate symptoms of mental illness.

By adopting a diet-based approach, Dr. Palmer began incorporating the ketogenic diet into his treatment plans for patients with different mental conditions. He conducted studies and observed promising results, including reductions in symptoms and improvements in overall well-being.

Dr. Palmer's work highlights the importance of considering nutrition as a potential addition or alternative to traditional treatments in mental health care. While medication and therapy remain essential components of treatment, the integration of dietary interventions offers a novel and complementary approach to improving mental health outcomes.

Additionally, Dr. Palmer has investigated the effects of the ketogenic diet on mitochondrial function. Mitochondria are the powerhouses of our cells, responsible for producing energy. Impaired mitochondrial function has been linked to various mental health disorders. Dr. Palmer's research suggests that the ketogenic diet may enhance mitochondrial function, potentially improving energy production and overall brain health.

He has also explored the effects of the ketogenic diet on stress and anxiety. Some of the studies suggest that the ketogenic diet may have a calming effect on the brain, potentially reducing stress and anxiety symptoms. By stabilizing blood sugar levels and promoting the state of ketosis, the diet may help regulate neurotransmitters and promote a sense of calm and well-being.

Practical steps to adopt a low carbohydrate diet.
1. It is important to Learn about the types of foods that are low in carbohydrates and free from refined sugars and refined carbohydrates. You need to familiarize yourself with the principles of the diet and understand which foods to include and which to avoid.

2. Find a diet that suits you and for that, you need to try various diets to determine which one suits you better.

3. Create a meal plan that focuses on whole, nutrient-dense foods. Include plenty of non-starchy vegetables, lean proteins, healthy fats, and moderate amounts of nuts, seeds, and low-sugar fruits. Avoid processed foods, sugary beverages, grains, and foods with added sugars.

4. If you're currently consuming a high-carbohydrate diet, consider gradually reducing your carbohydrate intake over time. This can help your body adjust and minimize potential side effects such as fatigue or cravings. Start by reducing refined sugars and carbohydrates, and gradually decrease your overall carbohydrate intake while increasing healthy fats and proteins.

5. Pay attention to food labels to identify hidden sources of refined sugars and carbohydrates. Ingredients like high-fructose corn syrup, white flour, and added sugars can be found in many processed foods. Opt for whole, unprocessed foods whenever possible. Rule of thumb, if it comes in a packet and has a label, it is not healthy.

6. Prepare your meals at home using fresh ingredients. This allows you to have control over the quality and composition of your meals. Experiment with new recipes and cooking methods to keep your meals interesting and enjoyable.

7. Consider joining online communities or finding support from friends or family members who are also following a low-carbohydrate diet. Sharing experiences, tips, and recipes can help you stay motivated and committed to your dietary goals.

8. Pay attention to how your body responds to the diet. Keep track of your energy levels, mood, and any changes in weight or body composition. Adjust your approach as needed to find what works best for you.

9. Be aware that the pleasant feeling or sensation we experience after eating is attributed to the release of the hormone dopamine. Understanding that it is dopamine we seek for emotional well-being, rather than food itself, can empower us to better manage the hormonal processes in our bodies. By recognizing that our desire for comfort or mood enhancement is related to dopamine, we can explore alternative ways to stimulate its release and find healthier ways to improve our emotional state.

10. Last but most importantly, make healthy eating a habit and integrate it into your identity. Once healthy eating becomes a regular part of your routine and aligns with your sense of self, it will be much easier to stay on track and resist foods that may be damaging to your well-being. By solidifying healthy eating as a core aspect of who you are, you can cultivate a strong foundation for making nourishing choices and maintaining a balanced lifestyle.

PILLAR III – STICK TO THE MISSION AND STRIVE FOR VICTORY

Stick to the mission and strive for victory is a core value that shapes the behavior and mindset of military leaders. It serves as a guiding light, emphasizing the significance of firm commitment to the mission and the pursuit of victory, regardless of the obstacles encountered.

This principle highlights the importance of staying focused on the mission at hand. Military leaders understand that a clear and well-defined mission provides a sense of purpose and direction. It serves as a compass, guiding their decision-making and actions. By adhering to the mission, leaders can effectively prioritize tasks, allocate resources, and ensure that every effort is aligned with the key goal.

Furthermore, the principle of striving for victory highlights the persistent pursuit of success. Military leaders know that victory is not always easily attained and that challenges and setbacks are certain. However, they maintain a firm determination to overcome these obstacles and achieve their objectives. This mindset of perseverance and resilience is crucial for leaders in any field. It enables them to navigate through adversity, learn from failures, and adapt their strategies to ultimately achieve success.

The principle of stick to the mission and strive for victory is not limited to the military domain. It is highly applicable to leaders from any walk of life. Whether in business, education, sports, or any other field, leaders can adopt this principle to drive their own success and inspire those around them.

For leaders in non-military contexts, applying this principle involves several key aspects. Firstly, it requires a deep commitment to a clear and meaningful mission or purpose. Leaders must define their goals and objectives, ensuring they align with their values and aspirations. This clarity of purpose provides a solid foundation for decision-making and action.

Secondly, leaders must cultivate resilience and perseverance. They should anticipate challenges and setbacks, understanding that they are part of the journey toward success. By maintaining a resilient mindset, leaders can navigate through difficulties, adapt their strategies, and keep moving forward.

Additionally, leaders should inspire and motivate others to strive for excellence. By embodying the principle of stick to the mission and strive for victory, leaders become role models for their teams. They set high standards, lead by example, and encourage others to give their best effort. This fosters a culture of continuous improvement and collective achievement.

During my time in the military, I was deeply drawn to the stick to the mission and strive for victory value. This value was exemplified by my commander "O", who represented them in every aspect of his leadership. His commitment to the mission and his persistent pursuit of victory inspired our entire team to perform at our best. Under his guidance, we achieved remarkable outcomes that exceeded expectations. It was through his living example that I truly understood the importance of these values for leadership and life in general.

Working alongside my commander, I witnessed firsthand how the value of striving for victory and sticking to the mission can transform a team's performance. His clear sense of purpose and solid determination encouraged a commitment to the mission. We were motivated to overcome challenges, adapt to changing circumstances, and push beyond our limits. The results we achieved as a team were evidence of the power of these values. I learned that embracing these values not only leads to success in the military but also has a profound impact on leadership and life outside of the army.

I would like to say that while stick to the mission and strive for victory is an important value, it is crucial to recognize that it should not be the sole focus of a leader or an organization. Instead, it should be complemented by a strong foundation of personal and organizational values and moral codes. These values guide our actions and decisions, ensuring that we achieve victory ethically and sustainably. By prioritizing integrity, respect, and ethical conduct before stick to the mission and strive for victory, we can navigate challenges and setbacks while staying true to our principles. Ultimately, it is through living by our values and moral codes that we can create a lasting impact and achieve meaningful success.

Why do leaders need to embrace the stick to the mission and strive for victory value?

Having a clear mission helps leaders stay focused on their goals and objectives. It provides a sense of direction and purpose, guiding decision-making and actions. When leaders stick to the mission, they can effectively prioritize tasks and allocate resources, ensuring that everyone is working towards a common goal.

Leaders who strive for victory inspire their teams to push beyond their limits and achieve exceptional results. By setting high standards and demonstrating a relentless pursuit of excellence, leaders motivate others to give their best effort. This creates a culture of continuous improvement and fosters a sense of purpose and fulfillment among team members.

Sticking to the mission and striving for victory require resilience in the face of challenges and setbacks. Leaders who embody this value demonstrate the ability to adapt to changing circumstances, learn from failures, and persevere toward their goals. This resilience inspires confidence and trust in their leadership, even during difficult times.

When leaders stick to the mission, they create a sense of alignment and unity within their teams. By clearly communicating the mission and its importance, leaders can rally their team members around a shared purpose. This fosters collaboration, cooperation, and a sense of belonging, leading to increased productivity and a stronger sense of camaraderie.

Leaders who consistently Stick to the Mission and Strive for Victory are more likely to achieve long-term success. By staying true to their vision and values, leaders can build a reputation for reliability, integrity, and consistency. This attracts talented individuals, loyal customers, and valuable partnerships, ultimately contributing to sustained growth and prosperity.

Academic Research

From an academic research perspective, the principle of stick to the mission and strive for victory holds significant importance and has notable effects on leadership and fulfillment. Numerous studies have highlighted the following points:

Goal Orientation and Leadership Effectiveness: Academic research, including studies by Judge et al. (2002) and Locke and Latham (2006), has consistently shown that leaders who demonstrate a strong commitment to achieving goals and maintaining focus on the mission tend to be more effective in motivating and guiding their teams towards success. This principle is associated with higher levels of leadership performance and fulfillment.

Motivation and Performance: Research, such as the studies by Judge et al. (2002) and Locke and Latham (2006), has demonstrated that setting clear and challenging goals, aligned with the mission, can enhance motivation, focus, and performance. Leaders who emphasize the importance of sticking to the mission and striving for victory create a sense of purpose and direction, leading to increased fulfillment and achievement.

Resilience and Determination: Academic studies, including those by Judge et al. (2002) and Locke and Latham (2006), have highlighted that leaders who stick to the mission and strive for victory exhibit resilience and determination in the face of challenges. This mindset fosters perseverance and a growth-oriented approach, enabling leaders to overcome obstacles and inspire their teams to do the same.

Organizational Success and Culture: Research, such as the studies by Judge et al. (2002) and Locke and Latham (2006), has shown that leaders who stick to the mission and strive for victory contribute to organizational success. Their unwavering commitment to the mission sets an example for others and helps shape a culture of excellence, achievement, and fulfillment within the organization.

Sense of Purpose and Fulfillment: Academic studies, including those by Judge et al. (2002) and Locke and Latham (2006), have highlighted that leaders who stick to the mission and strive for victory experience a greater sense of purpose and fulfillment. By pursuing challenging goals and achieving success, leaders find meaning in their work and inspire others to do the same.

These academic studies provide robust evidence supporting the importance and effects of the principles of sticking to the mission and striving for victory in leadership and fulfillment. By emphasizing these principles, leaders foster a sense of purpose, motivation, and achievement among their teams, leading to increased fulfillment and success.

Inspiring stories
Michael Jordan

Michael Jordan, widely regarded as one of the greatest basketball players of all time, exemplified an unmatched desire and commitment to excellence and victory throughout his career. Known for his persistent work ethic and competitive drive, Jordan consistently pushed himself to the limits, both physically and mentally. His mission to be the best, drove his dedication to continuous improvement, setting new standards for excellence in the sport. Whether it was his legendary scoring ability, defensive skills, or performances in crucial moments, Jordan's commitment to victory was evident in every aspect of his game.

What set Michael Jordan apart was not just his exceptional talent, but his firm commitment to victory. He possessed an incredible hunger for victory that drove him to push beyond his limits and inspire his teammates to do the same. Jordan's constant pursuit of excellence was evident in his preparation, his ability to rise to the occasion in high-pressure situations, and his belief in his own abilities. His competitive spirit and refusal to accept anything less than victory made him a true icon in the world of basketball, leaving a lasting legacy as a symbol of determination, resilience, and the pursuit of greatness.

Nelson Mandela

Nelson Mandela, an iconic figure in the fight against apartheid, exemplified the value of stick to his mission and strive for victory throughout his life. Despite facing immense adversity, Mandela remained true to his pursuit of a free and equal South Africa. His firm commitment to justice and equality led him to endure 27 years of imprisonment, during which he faced physical and emotional torture. Mandela's spirit and belief in his mission sustained him through the darkest times, inspiring not only his fellow prisoners but also people around the world.

Throughout his imprisonment, Mandela's determination to achieve his mission never stopped. He used his time in confinement to educate himself, engage in political discussions, and strengthen his purpose. Mandela's determination in the face of immense hardship became a symbol of hope and resilience for the oppressed and marginalized. His ability to maintain his focus on the mission of a free South Africa, even in the most challenging circumstances, showcased his extraordinary leadership and commitment to justice.

Lance Amstrong

Lastly, we will talk about a bittersweet example, Lance Amstrong, who lived by the stick to the mission and strive for victory value but decided to put aside other core values to achieve victory.

Lance Armstrong, a well-known bicycle champion, faced a tremendous battle against cancer and emerged as a symbol of resilience and determination. His winning mindset played a crucial role in his fight against the disease, as he refused to let it define or defeat him. Armstrong's belief in his ability to overcome challenges and his relentless pursuit of victory propelled him to not only survive cancer but also return to the world of professional cycling.

However, Lance Armstrong's legacy was damaged by his admission of cheating during his cycling career. Despite his remarkable triumph over cancer, Armstrong made the regrettable decision to compromise important values to achieve success in his cycling career. His use of performance-enhancing drugs damaged his achievements and betrayed the trust of his fans, fellow athletes, and the cycling community. This is a good reminder that even individuals with incredible talent and determination can, at times, prioritize victory over their core values, leading to very damaging consequences.

Practical ways to include the stick to the mission and strive for victory value into Practice.
1. Clearly define the mission and communicate it to your team. Ensure that everyone understands the purpose, goals, and objectives. Consistently reinforce the mission through team meetings, emails, and other communication channels.

2. Break down the mission into specific, measurable goals and milestones. This provides a roadmap for progress and allows you to track achievements along the way. Share these goals with your team and frequently review progress to stay on track.

3. Demonstrate your commitment to the mission and the pursuit of victory through your own actions. Show dedication, perseverance, and a positive attitude. Your team will be inspired by your example and be more motivated to follow.

4. Encourage individual and collective accountability within your team. Set expectations for performance and hold team members responsible for their contributions to the mission. Regularly provide feedback and recognize achievements.

5. When faced with challenges or setbacks, view them as opportunities for growth and learning. Encourage your team to analyze failures, identify lessons learned, and adjust strategies accordingly. Emphasize the importance of resilience and the ability to bounce back stronger.

6. Foster a collaborative environment where team members support

and help one another. Encourage open communication, idea sharing, and collaboration to overcome obstacles and achieve collective success.

7. Recognize and celebrate both small and significant victories along the way. This boosts morale, reinforces progress, and motivates your team to continue striving for success. Celebrations can be in the form of team acknowledgments, rewards, or even simple expressions of appreciation.

8. Regularly assess the alignment of your actions and strategies with the mission. Seek feedback from your team and stakeholders to ensure that you are on the right track. Be open to adjusting and refining as needed to stay aligned with the mission.

9. Continuously inspire and motivate your team by sharing success stories, providing positive reinforcement, and recognizing individual and collective efforts. Encourage a growth mindset and create opportunities for personal and professional development.

10. Demonstrate integrity, honesty, and transparency in your leadership. Build trust with your team by being open and transparent about challenges, decisions, and progress. This fosters a sense of trust and commitment to the mission.

PILLAR IV - EXERCISE

Exercise is not just about physical health or managing weight. It's about mental clarity, energy, and the ability to lead effectively. It's about fuelling our bodies and minds to make the best decisions, stay focused, and maintain the stamina to lead. Also, exercise can significantly contribute to our overall sense of fulfillment. It can boost our mood, improve our self-confidence, and provide a sense of accomplishment, all of which can improve our leadership effectiveness and personal satisfaction.

Throughout my career, exercise has played a significant role, particularly in my roles in the military and security services where physical fitness was a very important requirement. During these times, maintaining a regular exercise routine was not just about staying in shape, it was about being able to perform my duties effectively and efficiently.

However, there were times in my younger years when I didn't exercise regularly. Interestingly, I didn't notice a significant decline in my performance during these periods. But as I grew older, the impact of a sedentary lifestyle became more apparent. I experienced lower energy levels, decreased performance, and even periods of depression and anxiety. It was a stark contrast to the vitality and mental clarity I had when I was regularly exercising.

When I reintroduced regular exercise into my routine, the transformation was remarkable. I felt better overall, my energy levels increased, and my productivity improved. I found that I was making better decisions, both in my professional and personal life. Exercise became more than just a physical activity; it became a vital component of my leadership lifestyle and overall well-being.

Why exercise is so important for leadership?

Exercise plays a crucial role in leadership. One of the key reasons is its impact on cognitive functions. Regular physical activity has been shown to enhance memory, attention, and decision-making skills. These are all vital cognitive functions for effective leadership. Whether it's remembering important details about team members, staying focused during long meetings, or making strategic decisions, exercise can help leaders perform at their best. Moreover, exercise can boost energy levels, improving productivity and performance. In today's fast-paced business environment, leaders need to maintain high energy levels to keep up with the demands of their roles. Regular exercise, whether it's a morning jog or an afternoon gym session, can provide that much-needed energy boost.

In addition to increasing cognitive functions and energy levels, exercise can also help leaders manage stress. Leadership often comes with high levels of stress, which can take a toll on a leader's mental and physical health if not managed effectively. Exercise promotes the release of endorphins, the body's natural mood elevators. This can help leaders maintain a positive mindset, even in the face of adversity. It can also promote better sleep, which is essential for stress management and overall health.

Beyond these benefits for leadership, exercise can contribute significantly to personal fulfillment. It can improve self-confidence, providing a sense of accomplishment after each workout. This can translate into increased confidence in a leader's abilities, enhancing their leadership effectiveness. Exercise can also serve as a form of meditation, offering a break from the hustle and bustle of daily life. It provides an opportunity to disconnect, clear the mind, and focus on the present moment. This can foster a sense of inner peace and satisfaction, contributing to overall personal fulfillment. By fostering a healthier body and mind, regular exercise can enhance not only our leadership effectiveness but also our overall sense of well-being and satisfaction in life.

Types of exercise

There are several kinds of exercise that you can adopt to maintain high energy levels and improve cognitive functions and overall health. The kind of exercise you practice will depend on your fitness goals, time availability, fitness levels, and what kind of exercise you enjoy. These days There are a few types of exercises that are popular and recommended.

High-Intensity Interval Training (HIIT): This involves short bursts of intense exercise alternated with low-intensity recovery periods. For example, you might sprint for 30 seconds, then walk for 60 seconds, and repeat. HIIT workouts are typically quick and efficient, often lasting no more than 30 minutes. They can help improve cardiovascular fitness, increase metabolism, and burn fat.

Low-Intensity Steady State (LISS): This involves performing an activity at a low intensity but for a prolonged period. Examples include walking, light jogging, or cycling at a steady pace. LISS exercises are great for building endurance and can be easier on the body than high-intensity workouts.

Cardiovascular (Cardio) Exercise: This involves any exercise that increases your heart rate. Examples include running, cycling, swimming, or dancing. Cardio exercises can help improve heart health, increase lung capacity, and burn calories.

Resistance High-Intensity Interval Training (REHIIT): This is a variation of HIIT that incorporates resistance training. It involves short bursts of high-intensity resistance exercises (like weightlifting or bodyweight exercises) alternated with low-intensity recovery periods. REHIIT can help build strength and muscle, improve cardiovascular fitness, and burn fat.

Zone 2 Training: This involves performing an activity at a moderate intensity, typically 60-70% of your maximum heart rate. It's often used in endurance training and can help improve cardiovascular efficiency and fat burning. Examples include a steady-paced run, swim, or cycle.

Strength Training: This includes exercises that use resistance, like weightlifting or bodyweight exercises, to build muscle strength and endurance. It's essential for maintaining muscle mass, especially as we age, and can also help with weight management.

Yoga: This mind-body practice combines physical postures, breathing exercises, and meditation. It's recommended for its ability to improve flexibility, balance, and strength, as well as reduce stress and improve mental well-being.

Pilates: This low-impact exercise strengthens the core, improves posture, and increases body awareness. It's often recommended for its ability to improve overall body strength and flexibility.

Functional Fitness: These are exercises that train your muscles to work together and prepare them for daily tasks by simulating common movements you might do at home, at work, or in sports. It's recommended for improving balance, agility, and muscle strength, and reducing the risk of injuries.

Academic Research

Regular physical activity has been shown to enhance cognitive functions, including memory, attention, and executive functions, which are crucial for decision-making (Kramer & Erickson, 2007). Exercise stimulates the growth of new brain cells and helps prevent age-related decline (Colcombe & Kramer, 2003). It also improves neuroplasticity, the brain's ability to form and reorganize synaptic connections, especially in response to learning or experience (Voss et al., 2013). This means that regular exercise can help keep our brains flexible and adaptable, enhancing our ability to learn and remember new information.

Numerous studies have found a link between regular exercise and increased lifespan. Physical activity can help prevent chronic diseases, including heart disease, stroke, and type 2 diabetes, which are among the leading causes of premature death (Lee & Skerrett, 2001). Moreover, research has shown that even moderate exercise, such as walking for 30 minutes a day, can significantly reduce mortality risk (Ekelund et al., 2015). This underscores the importance of incorporating some form of physical activity into our daily routines for long-term health and longevity.

Exercise has been found to reduce symptoms of depression and anxiety and can help in the management of stress (Cooney et al., 2013). It promotes the release of endorphins, often known as the body's natural mood elevators. Additionally, exercise can act as a natural distraction from negative thoughts and can promote a sense of mastery and self-efficacy, further contributing to improved mental health (Craft & Perna, 2004).

Regular physical activity has been associated with improved decision-making abilities. Exercise can enhance blood flow to the brain, improve cognitive functions, and help maintain mental clarity, all of which can contribute to better decision-making (Hötting & Röder, 2013). In fact, a study by Chieffi et al. (2017) found that regular physical activity was associated with better performance on tasks requiring complex decision-making.

Exercise can also have significant benefits for social performance. Participating in group exercises or team sports can foster a sense of community, improve communication skills, and enhance teamwork (Eime et al., 2013). These social interactions can lead to improved social skills and relationships, which are crucial for effective leadership and personal satisfaction. Furthermore, physical activity can boost self-confidence (Babic et al., 2014), which can enhance social performance by making individuals more comfortable in social situations.

Frequent physical activity has been linked to improved emotional intelligence, which involves the ability to understand and manage our own emotions and those of others (Laborde et al., 2015). Exercise can promote better mood regulation, reduce stress, and improve mental clarity, all of which can contribute to greater emotional awareness and understanding. Moreover, the discipline and self-mastery associated with regular exercise can enhance our ability to manage our emotions effectively, a key aspect of emotional intelligence.

Inspiring Stories
Richard Branson
The founder of the Virgin Group is a strong advocate for physical fitness. He has often stated that his daily exercise routine, which includes activities like kite surfing, swimming, or weightlifting, gives him at least four additional hours of productive time each day. Branson believes that maintaining physical fitness helps him stay energetic and focused, enabling him to effectively manage his diverse global businesses. His commitment to fitness also aligns with his adventurous spirit and passion for life, which are key aspects of his personal brand and leadership style.

Barack Obama
During his presidency, he made physical fitness a priority despite his demanding schedule. He committed to working out for 45 minutes a day, six days a week, often starting his days with strength and cardio workouts. Obama has credited his exercise routine with helping him maintain stamina and focus, crucial for managing the pressures and responsibilities of leading a nation. His commitment to fitness also set a positive example for the nation, promoting the importance of a healthy lifestyle.

Indra Nooyi
The former CEO of PepsiCo is known for her early morning workouts. Despite the demands of leading a global corporation, she made physical fitness a priority. Nooyi believes that maintaining physical fitness helped her keep up with the demands of her role and stay focused and energized. Her commitment to fitness also reflects her belief in the importance of discipline and self-care, values that she promoted within her organization.

Mark Zuckerberg
Facebook CEO Mark Zuckerberg is known for setting personal challenges each year, many of which involve physical activity. For example,

he once set a goal to run 365 miles in a year. Zuckerberg has shared that running and other forms of exercise help him stay focused and motivated in his work. His commitment to fitness also reflects his belief in the importance of personal growth and continuous learning, principles that are at the core of Facebook's company culture.

Practical tips for incorporating Exercise into a leadership lifestyle.

1. Start Small: If you're new to exercising or getting back into it after a break, start with small, manageable goals. This could be a 10-minute walk each day or a few simple stretches in the morning. As your fitness improves, gradually increase the intensity and duration of your workouts.

2. Schedule It: Treat your workout like an important meeting. Schedule it into your day and make it non-negotiable. This can help ensure that you prioritize exercise, even on busy days.

3. Find Activities You Enjoy: You're more likely to stick with an exercise routine if you enjoy the activities. Try different types of exercise to find what you enjoy most, whether it's running, cycling, yoga, or weightlifting.

4. Mix It Up: Variety can keep your workouts interesting and help you stay motivated. Try to include a mix of cardio, strength training, and flexibility exercises in your routine.

5. Use the 'Two-Day Rule': Never skip exercising more than two days in a row. This rule can help you maintain consistency, which is key for establishing a regular exercise habit.

6. Make It Social: Exercising with a friend or group can make workouts more enjoyable and motivating. Consider joining a fitness class, sports club, or running group.

7. Listen to Your Body: Rest is important for recovery and preventing injuries. If you're feeling tired or sore, take a rest day or opt for a lighter workout. Remember, the goal is to make exercise a sustainable part of your lifestyle.

8. Make it a habit and part of your identity: The most important part of building a habit is consistency. Try to exercise at the same time each day to help it become a regular part of your routine. Also, Start thinking of yourself as someone who exercises regularly. This shift

in mindset can make it easier to stick with your routine.

PILLAR V – LEAD BY EXAMPLE

Leadership is not just about titles or positions; it's about influence and impact. And one of the most powerful ways to lead is by setting an example through our actions, behaviors, and values. When leaders lead by example, they create a ripple effect that resonates throughout their teams and organizations.

In the military, leading by example is not just a suggested approach; it is a deeply ingrained value that is vital to the success of military operations. The military recognizes that leaders who lead by example have a profound impact on the morale, cohesion, and effectiveness of their units. By embodying the behaviors, values, and principles they expect from their soldiers, leaders in the army inspire trust, foster discipline, and create a culture of excellence.

While leading by example is deeply embedded in the military, its principles extend far beyond the confines of the armed forces. The concept of leading by example is universally applicable and can be implemented in any organization, regardless of its industry or context. Whether it's a corporate setting, a nonprofit organization, or a small business, leading by example has the power to inspire, motivate, and drive great outcomes. By personifying the behaviors, values, and principles they expect from others, leaders in any organization can foster trust, accountability, and a positive work culture. Leading by example sets the tone for excellence, encourages teamwork, and empowers individuals to reach their full potential. It is a fundamental aspect of effective leadership that can create a ripple effect, transforming organizations and driving success.

On the other hand, when leaders fail to lead by example in an organization, it can have detrimental effects on the overall work environment and performance. Without a clear demonstration of expected behaviors and values, employees may become disengaged and lose trust in their leaders. This lack of trust can lead to a breakdown in communication, collaboration, and teamwork. In the absence of consistent and authentic leadership, employees may feel demotivated and uninspired, resulting in decreased productivity and a decline in the quality of work. Moreover, when leaders do not lead by example, it can create a culture of inconsistency and hypocrisy, where employees may feel a sense of unfairness and lack of accountability. Ultimately, the organization may experience higher turnover rates, decreased employee satisfaction, and a negative impact on its reputation.

During my time in the army, I learned firsthand the immense value of leading by example. In the military, it is not just a suggested approach; it is a deeply embedded value that permeates every aspect of our training and operations. I witnessed how leaders who led by example gained the respect and trust of their subordinates, fostering a strong sense of camaraderie and unity within the unit. Their actions spoke louder than words, and their unwavering commitment to the mission inspired us all to give our best. Through their demonstration of discipline, integrity, and dedication, they set the standard for excellence and motivated us to follow.

Practicing leading by example in the army and outside has been a transformative experience for me. By consistently embodying the values and behaviors I expected from my fellow soldiers and team members, I not only gained their respect but also witnessed the positive impact it had on our collective performance. When I led from the front, showing determination, resilience, and a strong work ethic, I noticed that my team members became more motivated and engaged. They were inspired to push beyond their limits and strive for excellence. The results were tangible - improved teamwork, increased productivity, and a shared sense of accomplishment. Leading by example not only felt great personally, but it also yielded great results for all involved.

What is Leading by Example
Leading by example is a leadership approach that involves setting a positive and influential example through one's actions, behaviors, and values. It is about embodying the principles and standards that we expect from others and inspiring them to follow. Leading by example is not limited to a specific industry or context; it is a fundamental aspect of effective leadership that transcends boundaries.

Leading by example in organizations goes beyond simply giving orders or delegating tasks. It involves actively participating in the work, showing empathy and respect towards others, and being transparent and authentic in communication. When leaders lead by example, they create an environment where individuals feel valued, motivated, and empowered to contribute their best.

By applying the principles of leading by example, leaders can cultivate a culture of excellence, continuous improvement, and fulfillment within their organizations. It sets the foundation for effective teamwork, innovation, and growth. When leaders consistently demonstrate the behaviors they expect from others, they create a ripple effect that inspires and influences their teams to strive for greatness.

Why leading by example is so important?
When leaders consistently demonstrate integrity, transparency, and ethical behavior, they earn the trust and respect of their employees. This fosters a positive work environment where open communication and collaboration thrive.

Leaders who actively participate in the work, show enthusiasm, and demonstrate a strong work ethic, inspire employees to do the same. Engaged employees are more committed, motivated, and willing to go the extra mile to achieve organizational goals.

Leaders who hold themselves accountable for their actions and decisions set a powerful example for others to follow. By demonstrating personal responsibility, they create a culture that fosters ownership and empowers employees to take charge of their work and outcomes.

When leaders exhibit positive attitudes, resilience, and a solutions-oriented mindset, it influences the overall atmosphere within the organization. A positive work culture increases employee satisfaction, well-being, and overall fulfillment.

Modeling effective leadership behaviors serves as a blueprint for aspiring leaders within the organization. By observing and learning from their leaders, employees are inspired to grow, develop their skills, and take on leadership roles in the future.

When leaders set high standards, demonstrate commitment, and actively support their teams, it motivates employees to strive for excellence. This leads to improved collaboration, productivity, and overall team performance.

Leaders who consistently embody the organization's vision, mission, and values, provide clarity and direction to employees, ensuring everyone is working towards a common purpose. This alignment fosters a sense of meaning and fulfillment in the work being done.

Embracing a growth mindset, taking calculated risks, and encouraging experimentation, creates an environment where employees feel empowered to think outside the box and contribute innovative ideas. This drives organizational growth and adaptability.

Prioritizing work-life balance, and self-care, and supporting employee well-being initiatives, sends a message that the organization values its employees' holistic success. This leads to higher job satisfaction and overall fulfillment.

Finally, when leaders consistently demonstrate the behaviors and values that drive success, it sets the tone for the entire organization. It creates a culture of excellence, continuous improvement, and fulfillment, which ultimately translates into achieving strategic goals and long-term success.

Academic Research

From an academic research perspective, the principle of lead by example holds significant importance and has notable effects on leadership and fulfillment. Numerous studies have highlighted the following points:

Trust and Credibility: Academic research has consistently shown that leaders who lead by example establish trust and credibility among their followers. Studies such as those by Mayer et al. (2019) and Walumbwa et al. (2008) have demonstrated that leaders who consistently demonstrate integrity, authenticity, and ethical behavior inspire confidence and create a foundation of trust.

Role Modeling: Research, including studies by Huang et al. (2016) and Bakker and Bal (2010), has consistently shown that leaders who lead by example serve as powerful role models for their followers. By embodying the values, behaviors, and qualities they expect from others, leaders set a standard of excellence and inspire their team members to emulate those traits.

Organizational Culture: Academic studies, such as those by Bakker and Bal (2010) and Huang et al. (2016), have highlighted that leaders who lead by example play a crucial role in shaping organizational culture. Their actions and behaviors influence the norms, values, and expectations within the workplace, contributing to the development of a healthy and supportive culture that promotes fulfillment and well-being.

Motivation and Inspiration: Research, including studies by Bakker and Bal (2010) and Mayer et al. (2019), has consistently shown that leaders who lead by example have a motivational and inspirational impact on their followers. By actively engaging in tasks and challenges, and demonstrating passion, resilience, and a strong work ethic, leaders motivate their followers to strive for excellence and achieve their full potential.

Ethical Decision-Making: Academic studies, such as those by Walumbwa et al. (2008) and Mayer et al. (2019), have highlighted that leaders who lead by example and exhibit ethical behavior positively influence the ethical decision-making processes of their followers. By consistently demonstrating honesty, fairness, and transparency, leaders create an ethical climate within the organization, encouraging followers to make ethical choices.

Employee Well-being and Satisfaction: Research, including studies by Bakker and Bal (2010) and Mayer et al. (2019), has consistently shown that leaders who lead by example have a positive impact on employee well-being and job satisfaction. By prioritizing work-life balance, self-care, and personal development, leaders create a supportive environment where individuals feel valued, cared for, and fulfilled in their work.

These academic studies provide robust evidence supporting the importance and effects of the principle of leading by example in leadership and fulfillment. By embodying the behaviors and qualities they wish to see in others, leaders create a positive and fulfilling work environment that promotes growth, success, and a sense of purpose for all.

Inspiring Stories
Mahatma Gandhi
The leader of the Indian independence movement is renowned for his commitment to nonviolent resistance and his unwavering dedication to his principles. He led by example through his own actions, practicing what he preached and living a simple and humble life. His selflessness, integrity, and perseverance inspired millions and played a pivotal role in India's struggle for independence.

Nelson Mandela
The former President of South Africa and anti-apartheid revolutionary demonstrated exceptional leadership by leading by example. During his 27 years of imprisonment, he remained steadfast in his commitment to equality, forgiveness, and reconciliation. After his release, he continued to embody these principles, promoting unity and reconciliation in South Africa.

Mandela's ability to forgive and his unwavering dedication to justice and equality made him an iconic leader.

Mother Teresa
Catholic nun and humanitarian. She dedicated her life to serving the poor and marginalized. She led by example through her selfless acts of compassion and love. Mother Teresa lived among the people she served, providing care, comfort, and support to those in need. Her humility, kindness, and unwavering commitment to her mission continue to inspire people around the world.

Malala Yousafzai
Pakistani activist for female education and the youngest Nobel Prize laureate has shown remarkable leadership by leading by example. Despite facing threats and violence, she fearlessly advocated for girls' education and women's rights. Yousafzai's courage, resilience, and determination have inspired countless individuals worldwide to stand up for what they believe in and fight for equality and education.

These examples highlight leaders who have made a significant impact by leading through their actions, values, and principles. They have inspired others, created positive change, and left a lasting legacy. By leading by example, these leaders have shown the power of authenticity, integrity, and selflessness in driving meaningful transformation.

Practical Strategies for leading by example
1. Clearly communicate your expectations to your team members. Be specific about the behaviors, values, and standards you want to see demonstrated. When expectations are clear, it becomes easier for everyone to align their actions with the desired outcomes.

2. Be true to yourself and your values. People are more likely to follow a leader who is genuine and transparent. Embrace your strengths and weaknesses, and show vulnerability when appropriate. This authenticity will inspire trust and create a positive work environment.

3. Hold yourself accountable for your actions and decisions. Admit mistakes when they happen and take responsibility for them. By demonstrating accountability, you set the tone for your team to do the same. This fosters a culture of ownership and continuous improvement.

4. Actively listen to your team members and show genuine interest in their ideas, concerns, and feedback. This demonstrates respect and fosters open communication. When you listen attentively, you encourage others to do the same, creating a culture of collaboration and mutual respect.

5. Show a commitment to personal and professional growth. Continuously seek opportunities to learn and develop new skills. Share your knowledge and experiences with your team, and encourage them to pursue their own growth. By being a lifelong learner, you inspire others to do the same.

6. Maintain a positive attitude, even in challenging situations. Your attitude sets the tone for the team and influences their morale. By staying positive and optimistic, you inspire others to approach obstacles with resilience and find solutions.

7. Show your team that it is possible to prioritize personal well-being while still achieving professional success. Encourage your team members to take breaks, prioritize self-care, and maintain a healthy work-life integration.

8. Acknowledge and appreciate the efforts and achievements of your team members. Celebrate their successes and publicly recognize their contributions. By showing appreciation, you create a positive and supportive work environment that motivates and inspires others.

9. Be clear, transparent, and consistent in your communication. Keep your team informed about important updates, changes, and decisions. Encourage open and honest communication, and be receptive to feedback. Effective communication builds trust and fosters a culture of collaboration.

10. Finally, lead by doing. Be actively involved in the work, demonstrate the behaviors you expect from others, and be willing to roll up your sleeves and get your hands dirty. By actively participating, you show your team that you are not just a leader in title but also a leader in action.

Remember, leading by example is an ongoing practice. It requires consistency, self-awareness, and a genuine commitment to living your values. By implementing these practical strategies, you can inspire and motivate your team to reach their full potential and create a positive and fulfilling work environment.

EPILOGUE

As we reach the end of this journey exploring the five pillars of fulfilling leadership, we find ourselves standing at the precipice of transformation. Throughout this book, we have delved into the depths of service to others and a purpose, the significance of a balanced diet, the power of sticking to the mission and striving for victory, the importance of exercise, and the impact of leading by example. These pillars have provided us with a solid foundation upon which to build our leadership and pursue a life of fulfillment.

But now, dear reader, it is time to take action. It is not enough to simply understand the principles; we must embody them in our daily lives and leadership practices. It is through action that we truly bring about change and make a lasting impact on ourselves and those around us.

Let us commit to serving others and a higher purpose, seeking opportunities to make a positive difference in the lives of those we encounter. Let us nourish our bodies and minds with a balanced diet, recognizing the profound connection between our well-being and our ability to lead effectively. Let us stay true to our mission, unwavering in our pursuit of victory, and resilient in the face of challenges.

Physical exercise must become a non-negotiable part of our routines, as we understand that a healthy body supports a healthy mind and enhances our capacity to lead. And let us lead by example, embodying the values, behaviors, and qualities we wish to see in others, inspiring and empowering those around us to reach their full potential.

As we embark on this path of fulfilling leadership, let us remember that it is not a destination but a continuous journey. We will face setbacks, obstacles, and moments of doubt. But it is in these moments that our commitment to the five pillars will be tested, and it is through perseverance and resilience that we will emerge stronger and more fulfilled.

So, dear reader, I encourage you to take action. Reflect on the insights gained from this book and identify the areas where you can implement the principles of fulfilling leadership in your own life. Start small, but start today. Embrace the power of service, nourishment, focus, movement, and leading by example. Let these pillars guide you as you navigate the complexities of leadership and strive for a life of purpose and fulfillment.

Remember, you have the capacity to make a profound impact on the world through your leadership. Embrace the five pillars, embody them with passion and conviction, and watch as your leadership and fulfillment soar to new heights. The world is waiting for your unique contribution. Now, go forth and lead with purpose, my friend.

www.ingramcontent.com/pod-product-compliance
Lightning Source LLC
Chambersburg PA
CBHW062258290526
45794CB00006B/2608